THE 10 THINGS

AN INVITATION TO DIVE IN

MIMI SCHLICHTER

The 10 Things: An invitation to dive in
Copyright ©2017
by Mimi Schlichter

All rights reserved, including the right
of reproduction
in whole or in part in any form.
For permission requests,
please contact the author.
MimisArt.com

First edition, Mimi's Art 2017

Artist photo by VagabondView Photography

Cover design by Chrissy Caskey

Cover photo by Mimi Schlichter

Schlichter, Mimi
THE 10 THINGS: An invitation to dive in
ISBN 978-0-9963308-2-4

for... well, you know who you are

"It's great being here on Sunday morning, but how do I get more God into my life during the week?"

That was the question asked of me by a friend after worship service one Sunday morning not too long ago. We talked briefly on the spot, then a bit more by phone on the drive home.

Fueled perhaps by too much caffeine earlier in the day, though hopefully Spirit led and inspired, I found myself with notebook and pen in hand at 12:23am, writing a letter about what had worked for me in my own faith journey. Whether what I did would work for someone else, I didn't know. I just knew I had to write it down before I could sleep.

What follows is the essence of that letter, with only minimal editing.

Please know from the start that I am not a theologian, nor do I pretend to be one. I'm simply someone working my way through life, full of questions, perhaps similar to you, hoping for a closer walk with God.

A lifelong Lutheran, I started attending an Evangelical Christian church a little over two years ago. A friend had told me about the place, but I simply could not imagine myself worshiping at a Baptist church. Until I hit a personal "rock bottom" and found myself feeling particularly lonely, and in need of some extra help one Sunday morning.

I walked into that church on November 9, 2014, truly skeptical, thinking, *"yeah, right, show me what you've got."* I fully expected to be disappointed or perhaps even angered by what I might hear. Instead, I found myself in a puddle of tears at the end of the pastor's message, titled "The Beauty of Emptiness." It was as if God was speaking directly to me, to where I sat in life at that moment. Through my tears I sent a one word text to my friend. *"Wow."* To which I believe the response was a polite version of *"I told you so."*

I was hooked.

I suppose my personal theology might now be considered a hybrid. Liberal feminist who testifies to having been saved by Jesus Christ and baptized at age 55, loving and living life in a whole new way. Haven't changed my politics. Though I have changed a whole lot of other things in my life.

You don't have to agree with what I say. And please, I am not looking for an argument.

This is simply what came to me late one night, penned longhand in a letter to a friend. I think it is worth sharing.

The Letter

10/10/16 - 12:23am.

Can't sleep because the conversations from earlier today, at church, and in the car, are rolling around in my head.

IF you are serious, deep down in your bones serious, about wanting to grow closer to God, and if you are willing to listen, I would like to share with you what I have found worked for me in this past year.

It isn't easy, the faith walk, because it means letting go of a bunch of old habits and patterns, and going against society "normal."

Ok. Here goes.

1) Got down on my knees and SURRENDERED. Said *"I give up Lord, I can't do this alone. I NEED you in my life. Not just want, but need."* It meant giving up control. And trusting God.

Surrendered my life to God. It's no longer about me. None of this ever was mine to begin with. It's God's. God gives us life. It's up to us to give it back. All for Him.

2) I had to be prepared to make some tough choices. For me, it meant giving up alcohol (it fogs the clarity of a connection with God, and you've seen what a mess it makes of me). Meant giving up going out to bars with friends, and giving up some friends who didn't fit. And yes, swearing. And casual sex. Not that I did that much of that, but you know what I'm talking about.

3) Surround myself with reminders. I listen to Christian music now in my car and at home. K-Love radio. Try it. Their tag is "positive, encouraging, K-love." It reminds me of who is at the center of my day.

I read books that relate to faith. The Bible, and other. Even have changed what I watch in movies and television. Some might call it brainwashing. I suppose it is. All I know is that what I was doing before wasn't working, so why not?

If I want my life to change for the better, it means I need to be willing to make some changes in how I live my life. A changed life can't and won't happen by holding on to old routines that left me feeling empty.

4) Get back down on my knees again and again. (*Now you understand the holes in the knees of my jeans!*) Ask for help in every situation all day long. Then listen, and pay attention, and do my best to be willing to follow it. A tough work situation? I pray silently for help. A difficult personal situation, or challenged to do something I know isn't right, I pray for a way out. Then watch it show up. This isn't magic mumbo jumbo, but God IS supernatural.

5) I have to be WILLING. Willing to give up some things. Maybe a lot of things. It's not easy, but the reward is amazing.

6) Surround myself with friends on a similar path. Church "small group" helps with that. Having opportunity to talk with others also seeking to be closer in

their walk with God. Drinking and hanging out with bar flies doesn't help me to grow.

7) I'm learning to be prepared for opposition. I never used to believe there was an evil one, but in the past year have begun to realize the strength of opposition it throws at me. *(Ephesians 6:10-20)* Every time I start to feel like *"yes, I've got this - I feel God's presence - this is amazing"* - the opposition shows up in the form of doubts, fears, and temptation to old patterns. That's when having other Christian friends to talk to is powerful.

8) Have you really truly invited God into your heart? I used to hear about it, and it sounded corny to me, until I experienced it.

PLACE GOD CENTRAL AND ABSOLUTE NUMBER ONE PRIORITY IN YOUR LIFE.

A constant companion. I talk with God all day, every day. Some call it prayer. I just think of it as an ongoing conversation with the very best friend ever.

Say thank you. Be amazed by what God is able to do. Allow God to work through you to be a light in the lives of other people. Not the fake type we sometimes do as part of our job, but true, genuine caring. I know you have it in you - I've seen it. Remember - it's not about you anymore, if you really want to embrace this path of life.

9) I got down on my knees again. Was silent. Listened. Continued to be willing

to do the tough things. Like holding my tongue when I want to tell someone off. Or not casting judgment on someone else. Or simply listening when I would rather run off with my own thoughts (that one is harder than it sounds).

10) And forgive myself. I'm a work in progress. I don't always get it right, but I keep trying.

There's probably more, but I need to sleep. Couldn't do so with all of this rolling in my head.

So I'll close with this.

Your life choices are up to you. Get down on your knees. Stop trying to "figure it out" (words I have deleted from my vocabulary) and allow God to show you the way.

Surrender - real surrender - is in the same breath the most difficult thing to do and the easiest thing to do.

Because when we let go, and invite God into our lives, all sorts of amazing things can and will happen.

1 Corinthians 10:12-13. If you think you are standing strong, be careful not to fall. The temptations in your life are no different from what others experience. And God is faithful. He will not allow the temptation to be more than you can stand. When you are tempted, he will show you a way out so that you can endure.

The 10 Things

I shared the letter with a couple of friends, and asked what they thought of it. Their response was, *"Love it! But I want to know more. A bit more explanation on each of your points."* Or as one friend said, *"put some clothes on the skeleton!"*

Which, quite honestly, places me in a quandary. Because my intention is that this piece stays small and to the point, as close as possible to what I wrote that night. Something to be read quickly at first, and re-visited later. An invitation to inquiry, and discussion.

So, here is my compromise.

The letter stands as written. In hindsight there are some things I might say differently, other things I might add. But to do so would lose the original inspiration that consumed me that night. So I have refrained from editing.

Rather, in the following pages I will explore each point just a little further.

I still want to keep this simple. Trust that Spirit will speak to you through my words, wherever you are in your own inquiry.

I begin with a prayer. *"Please, God, inspire my words that they might serve others in their own faith walk. If they help to move just one person closer to you, then this is worthwhile."*

1. The Surrender Thing. How do I let go of my own wants and make space for God to show me the way? My personal preference is to kneel on my knees beside my bed, with my head bowed in my hands, as I talk with God. *"I surrender my life to you, God. I'm ready for it to not just be about me any more. That hasn't gone so well. I want a better way. I want my life to have meaning and purpose. I ask you, God, what is it you want me to do with my life? Lead me. Guide me. Please."*

It's kind of silly, really, to think of "giving" my life to God. Has way too much personal ego in it. If I believe God to be creator of all, then God created me, and all that I have, and all that I am. It's all God's already. I'm simply acknowledging and accepting this, surrendering in the true sense of the word. Consider something like this…

"I give up, God. I'm tired of trying to do this my way. I'm ready to attempt to put my own selfish pride aside and follow you."

2. The Tough Choices Thing. While God's love for me doesn't depend on my actions - God's grace is a gift - the choices I make can witness to my gratitude for that love, and my respect for who God is in my life.

How I act. What I do with my time. And with my body.

We complicate it, like we're not really sure what the right thing is to do, or not do.

But c'mon now. Let's just be real simple and honest here. This is God we're talking about. Think about it this way.

If Jesus was here with you, right now, you would know what things you do that you want him to see, and what things you would rather hide. Yes, it's that simple. Just try to make decisions as if Jesus is sitting right next to you, your best friend riding along with you in all you do. You know in your heart what to keep, and what to let go of, don't you?

Let me get a little silly about this for those of you who are still wrestling with the whole idea of Jesus, and maybe not comfortable with the idea of him sitting next to you. Shift it to Santa Claus. His "naughty and nice" list. Imagine Santa Claus is riding with you all day, and sees everything you do, and knows everything you say.

You've got this now, don't you?

And no, for those of you who are sitting horrified right now because you think I just made Santa Claus and Jesus Christ the same person, that is not what I said. But it helped you get the idea, didn't it?

3. The Reminder Thing. I read books on faith, but I'm a slow reader, and a visual person, so I also place reminders in places where I can see them.

In those first and last few precious moments of the day, when taking mental inventory of what lies ahead, and what's been, it's a wonderful thing to be reminded that I am forgiven.

My baptismal certificate is framed and hangs on the wall in my bedroom so that it is the first thing I see when I wake up in the morning and the last thing I see before I go to sleep at night.

I've posted small signs on my fridge and bathroom mirror with words like "trust" and "patience." Written Bible verses on Post-it notes, stuck inside the cabinet over the sink to read while brushing my teeth. Used a dry erase pen on the side of the refrigerator door the other day to remember something I heard on the television.

Is it brain washing? As I heard one person say, *"Sure - why not? What rolled around in my head before was ugly and dirty. Why not wash it clean and replace it with lighter, brighter thoughts?"* And I'm not talking power of positive thinking type stuff. This is about prayer, and the Bible, and making room for my thoughts to be inspired so that the words I say and the things I do might be uplifting to others.

4. The Ask for Help Thing. Ah, the prayer thing again. "On my knees" has become the place I go when I feel overwhelmed, confused, angry, or scared. Truthfully, I need to remember to do it more often, because when I do, God is always there for me without fail.

It's like having a best friend who will pick up the phone each and every time I call and always knows exactly the right thing to say. It might not be the thing I want to hear, but it is always, without fail, what is best for me. How cool is that?

That's all prayer is, you know. At its most basic, it is simply a conversation with God. Talking and listening. Try it. *"Hey God, it's me. Might we please talk for a few minutes?"* It can start that easily.

5. The Willing Thing. This is just another component of the surrender thing. If I am going to trust God and pray for direction, then I need to be willing to do what God asks of me. I can't truly surrender with my fingers crossed behind my back.

Which leads to the challenging question of how to recognize God's voice. As for me, I pray for discernment, wisdom, and the courage to follow. Then I practice with little choices and decisions. Ask. Listen. Follow. Watch what happens. Miracles in little things.

I ask God for signs, and God delivers. I know God is at work in my life all the time, but when I see and feel evidence of it in real life, what some call God winks, it brings a ridiculous grin to my face. It is amazing. Beyond description.

There are likely some who will want to debate me in this area. Who am I to suggest that I hear God respond to my prayers, or that I receive signs? Please remember I am simply sharing with you out of my own experience. And honestly I don't think it is that far reaching an idea. I pray to God with questions. Why not expect responses?

6. The Friends Thing. The company we keep is important. I will warn you that this path, living with God central and number one in your life, is not an easy one to follow. On occasion it defies logic, and certainly goes against a lot of society norms and expectations.

I'm not suggesting you position yourself as someone better than others because you have decided to surrender your life to God, or that you abandon your current friends. I do suggest that you seek out some new friends on a similar path, with whom you can talk about and celebrate how you feel and experience God in the midst of your life.

I will also suggest that it is ok to draw appropriate boundaries with those who might tempt you to go back to old patterns or habits that no longer serve. My experience has been that I can't move forward with my feet in two different places. I can't expect new life with God while still doing the things that belonged to the old life.

7. The Enemy Thing. Oh my, this one is huge. More than I ever knew. Didn't believe it was real. Now I do.

Be prepared when it shows up. It can be sly and subtle.

The enemy wants you to be ruled by your ego, and to be interested in the great race for "more." More stuff. More fame. More personal glory. Anything to distract you from your decision to live with God in the center of your life.

The big stuff is easy to notice. The subtle stuff will sneak up on you. "Cheating just a little bit" is still cheating. A "white lie" is still a lie.

When you feel yourself slipping, hold on to God that much more. Say the name of Jesus out loud. Ask God to intervene. God is always able, always stronger. Pay attention. Be prepared.

For the past couple of years, almost without fail, after a time when I would feel particularly close to God, I would experience a sort of backlash, what I used to think was a testing coming from God. Then there was an ah-ha moment, and I began to look at the same situations through a different lens.

It occurred to me that those "tests" might actually be challenges from the enemy. A darker voice saying, *"So, you think you've got this God thing working in your life? Well, let's try this circumstance and see how you do."*

I am working to embrace those times not as challenges against my faith, but rather as opportunities to draw that much closer to God. *(James 4:7-8)*

When you feel challenged, invite God into the situation. Ask for help.

Remember, you are never alone. God is ALWAYS with you to help you.

8. The Invitation Thing. I like the simplicity of what I wrote in the original letter about this one, but I suppose I need to say a little more. I just want to share with you how I experienced it - being saved by Jesus Christ.

In truth it happened over an extended period of time, but culminated in a defining moment one Sunday morning. The pastor preached a message that asked the question, "do you believe the resurrection was real?" It is a question of great importance because it sets Christianity apart from anything else one might call spiritual. In that moment of acknowledging it as real, we open our hearts to being able to accept God's forgiveness and invite Jesus Christ into our lives.

Some will say the grace is given as a gift from God, and it does not require an action from me to accept it. Which puts us on the edge of theological debate. All I can tell you is what happened to me.

I came home that Sunday after church, after hearing the message with the question, and laid down for a nap. Before I did, I prayed a very simple prayer. Something like this. *"Dear God, I want to believe this is real, but I'm just not sure. Can you give me a sign please? If this is real can you show me?"*

I awoke from that nap in a puddle of tears, with a heart that felt more full of love than I had ever known in my previous 55 years. And I knew that so many years of searching for perfect love from another human had been in vain - because I was looking for a person to fill the hole in my heart that could only be filled by God.

That was August 30, 2015. Life has not been the same since. Not perfect. Still often challenging. But I KNOW now that I am NEVER alone. And that is a VERY cool thing.

9. The Again Thing. The more we know, the more we realize we don't know. So it's back on the knees, asking God again, and again, and again. And I am so grateful that God is patient with me, because I know I have stretched beyond reasonable in the number of times I have asked certain questions. It's ok. God can take it. Broader shoulders and more patience than anyone I know here on earth.

10. The Forgiveness Thing. Just because "I knew it" on August 30, 2015 doesn't mean I've got this thing all set in my life. I'm human. I'm a work in progress. I backslide. I make mistakes. I get stubborn and tired and impatient and throw temper tantrums. I want things to be the way I want them to be.

I need to allow myself to be human. I slip up, or forget, or just become downright defiant and say *"I don't feel like doing this anymore."* And God forgives me. I get up the next day, and start all over again. Sometimes I need to lighten up, and be cautious I don't place unreasonable expectations on myself. That's just the enemy, setting me up for a fall. Instead, I need to embrace my human nature as yet another reason to draw that much closer to God.

Because even when I mess up, God is here, arms open wide, ready to love me.

It's unconditional love at its finest. I thought my dog was good at it but God's love is even better. Every time I wake up to my own weaknesses, afraid to try again, God is here. Every time I think I've got this thing and then go and do exactly the opposite thing, God is here. No matter how very good I am at getting in my own way, God is here.

And just one more thing...

The Bible. I invite you to allow God to speak to you through the words of Scripture. I begin every day with it. There's an app if you prefer. I suggest The Bible App. I like the "Verse of the Day." I find it to be a lovely way to set the tone for my day.

THE ONE THING

The most important thing:

God loves you more than you can likely even begin to conceive, not because of what you do, or don't do, but simply for being who you are. There is nothing you can ever do to change God's heart.

No matter what life throws your way, no matter how dark or lost you might feel, please never ever give up. Pray *(talk with God.)* Ask for help. And allow yourself to feel God's love in your life. It won't necessarily make your problems go away, or suddenly fill your bank account, or cure an illness. But God's pure love for you, and accepting God's love and grace, I promise you, it changes everything.

The Invitation

Please remember... I'm not a theologian. I have a liberal arts degree from a small college, with a major in biology, though probably should have studied art or music or just about anything other than biology. I've never taken a creative writing class, and avoided English literature courses. I write simply because I have thoughts and life experiences I want to share that I think might be of help to others.

So what qualifies me to write? Perhaps just the fact that I'm so ridiculously over the top grateful to God for saving me from the collision course I was on by myself. It wasn't big stuff that I messed up, just a whole lot of little things that added up to a mess. (Well there was one big thing, but that's a different story.)

I thank you for reading this, for whatever reason you chose to entrust and share with me a few minutes of your life.

And most importantly, if you haven't already, I invite you to give this thing a try. What have you got to lose? Invite Jesus Christ into your heart, into your life. Such a simple prayer - one that changes everything.

May you come to know and experience the fullness of God's love in your own life.

Mimi

PS. This isn't just about you.

God's love is a precious gift. It's meant to be shared.

Extend your own invitations to others to experience God's love. And don't just tell them your life has changed. Show them by how you live.

Then be ready to feel your own faith grow as you watch others blossom.

Because while experiencing God's love personally is awesome, sharing it with someone else, and seeing their life change in beautiful ways - oh wow - there is absolutely nothing like it.

John 13:34 I give you a new commandment, that you love one another. Just as I have loved you, you also should love one another.

I thank God for the life path and inspiration that created this book, and for each and every friend who supports, encourages, and shares with me in this faith journey.

Mimi Schlichter is an
artist, author, and musician.
She is passionate about
faith, family, and friends.

Full bio online at MimisArt.com
Blog at TheSacredThings.com

www.ingramcontent.com/pod-product-compliance
Lightning Source LLC
Chambersburg PA
CBHW050547300426
44113CB00012B/2298